This Journal Belongs To:

Name ....

Email ....

Telephone ....

Breathe

Mindfulness

JOURNAL

STERLING
New York

Mindfulness

The word is everywhere these days, but here at *Breathe*, the original mindfulness magazine, we think it's more than just another fad. Chances are, if you've picked up this journal, you're looking for a little space and peace, some time away from everyday pressures and the racing thoughts that can add to that stress. And this is where mindfulness comes in—it can be a powerful tool, helping you to notice negative thought patterns and break their cycle, giving you the freedom to face today's busy world with calmness and clarity.

Brought to you by the creators of *Breathe*, this journal is a collection of features mindfully curated just for you. It's filled with brand-new, simple exercises that can be done wherever you are—on the train, during your lunch break, or curled up on the couch at home. Carry it with you and use it to bring mindfulness into your daily life. Don't feel you need to read it in any particular order. Adapt and make the exercises relevant to you. Skip things, do some more than once, and add your own. Beautifully illustrated, with space to record your innermost thoughts and ideas, this journal is your body-and-soul guide to a relaxed, more fulfilled you.

Breathe

breathemagazine.com

Contents

Live for the moment

*Being creatures of habit, many people live their lives on autopilot.
But sometimes you need to turn off your internal route plotter
and be fully in the moment.*

Everyone has an autopilot. It is formed from habitual learning—a process where
behaviors become automatic through regular repetition. Your brain hardwires
things you do on a repetitive basis so you can do them again without needing
much thought, making you more efficient.

Have you ever driven to work and been completely lost in thought? Although
you arrive safely, the journey itself is at best somewhat hazy as you struggle
to recall the songs you listened to, the roads you drove down, or obstacles and
hazards you had to avoid. While you're physically present, you're not consciously
thinking about what it is you're doing. As your mind disengages from the present
moment, it becomes free to wander aimlessly. This can be a very useful and
adaptive skill to have at times, serving you well, but there are drawbacks
to relying on this automated mode to guide you through life.

Three problems with being on autopilot

1 The first is spending too much time on it. Experts say people are on
autopilot—meaning they're not in full control—for almost half of their lives.
When people's minds are left free to wander, they tend to find themselves stuck
in the past or imagining future scenarios. Often these thoughts veer toward
negativity and can become destructive and distracting, leading to anxiety and
worry. People become disconnected from the present moment and reality itself.
As a result, they can flitter over big chunks of their lives, often the good parts
that should be cherished—like watching your child in a school play, but thinking
about your to-do list for work tomorrow. People become caught in a quest of
surviving the day or going through the motions, and before they know it they
hit retirement and are left thinking: "Where did all that time go?"

2 The second problem is that when you let your automated mode take over the controls, you end up taking the same old familiar route you've gone down in the past—repeating the same habits, patterns, rituals, and routines. At some point these may have served you well, but now they may not be your best option. As a result, you can end up experiencing the same problems again and again, and fail to move on with your life.

3 When you get caught up in your thoughts, feelings, and emotions, your brain reacts automatically without thinking. Although people's ability to react swiftly helped them to survive in prehistoric times—such as bolting from a saber-toothed tiger—in today's modern world, it can prevent you from responding in constructive ways that bring out your best. Say you're driving along a road. Out of nowhere, a car cuts in front of you. You impulsively react, cursing under your breath. Although you don't know the reason why the person pulled out, your mind—which was distracted by thoughts of what you have or haven't done or are going to do—makes a snap judgment, causing you to think only negative things of the driver and react angrily.

Who's driving this bus?

So, shouldn't you try to grab back the controls, awaken your senses, and install focus and intention back into your life, so you appreciate all that you have? With training and the aid of mindfulness, you can become more in tune with your body and mind, noticing when you are on autopilot, while having the power to switch it off when it's not benefiting you—when it creates needless worry and fear, when you get stuck in old habits, or when it doesn't bring out your best.

Act with awareness

By interrupting autopilot through mindfulness, your mind becomes fully engaged in the present moment—with full awareness, focus, and activation of your senses. When thoughts, feelings, and emotions arise, you don't cling on to them or try to block them out. Instead, you just observe and acknowledge them—without judgment or criticism—accepting them, letting them be, and noticing how they slowly subside. Choosing how to respond, you act with awareness.

So, while autopilot takes you away from your life, mindfulness has the power to bring you back into it. By practicing mindful techniques, you can change the hardwiring of your brain, enabling you to spend more time truly living in the moment; to create new healthy habits to live by; to make better choices; and to grow into the highest version of yourself.

Turn off the autopilot

Try the following six mindful ways to switch off your autopilot.
Practice them any time, any place, and record your thoughts.

1. Take a mindful walk

Instead of driving, why not go for a mindful walk? People tend to lose touch with their bodies on autopilot. Mindful movement offers reconnection. As you walk, become aware of every small movement you make—your heel lifting, knee bending, toes curling, foot moving forward and resting back on the ground. Once you have settled into a rhythm, start to bring your awareness into your body.

How does it feel?

....
....
....
....

Which parts are holding tension?

....
....
....
....

What is your breathing like?

....
....
....

Just observe, without trying to change anything. Then shift your focus to your external environment. Activate all your senses as you take in the sights, smells, sounds, and touch of your surroundings. What do you notice?

2. Set up auto-triggers

With life on autopilot, it's easy to find yourself going through the motions, day-in, day-out. To snap out of this mode, establish some auto-triggers. Set up alarms on your phone or computer to go off at certain intervals throughout the day. Give them a description that says: "Time to be more mindful." Every time the alarm goes off, take a moment for yourself, fully activate all of your senses, read the words, and ask:

Where are you?

....

....

....

....

....

....

How are you feeling?

....

....

....

....

....

....

What is your breathing like?

....

....

....

....

....

....

3. Create mind gaps

In between one thought and another there is a gap, otherwise known as a mind gap. This is your natural state of self where you're fully alert, aware, and present in the moment. Try to create a mind gap next time you go about one of your daily tasks. Give your full attention to what it is you're doing, using all of your senses. If thoughts pop into your head, just observe and acknowledge them. Don't try to attach meaning or react. As they pass, bring awareness to the empty spaces that form and enjoy the silent sense of presence. At first, you may experience them only for a short period of time; this is because of your inherent need to fill in silences. In time, they will become longer.

4. Do that thing you've been putting off

On autopilot, people tend to procrastinate and avoid doing things they really don't want to do for as long as possible. How many times have you put off something, but been left with that horrible feeling of dread as you know you have to get it done at some point? You keep pushing it to the end of your to-do list, hoping it will magically disappear or someone will take it off your plate. Next time, move the item you are dreading to the top of your list and make time in your diary so you can strike it off as soon as possible.

This mindful exercise can improve your ability to focus and recover from distraction.

- Sitting or standing, take a deep breath and close your eyes. Let your arms rest loosely by your sides. Relax your shoulders.

- Breathe in slowly through your nose and blow the air gently out of your mouth. As you finish exhaling, count one.

- Continue slowly breathing in and out, up to the count of 10.

- Each time your mind wanders, notice where it goes before gently bringing your attention back to the breath.

Try to practice this exercise for five minutes a day, for a week. How does it feel to spend some time each day simply with your breath?

5. Be aware of how you use digital communication

Today's technology means you are constantly connected to those around you. When you have a break in the day, it's easy to start flicking mindlessly through social media, checking emails, or communicating with others. Living this way means you're never truly on your own or fully present. But cutting out technology entirely is often impractical. Instead, focus on becoming more aware of your motivations and emotions when you use it.

When do you look at your phone or emails? (*As soon as you wake up; late at night; while you're with friends.*)

....

....

....

....

....

How does it make you feel when you use it? (*Connected; isolated; happy; anxious.*)

....

....

....

....

....

What effect does it have on different aspects of your life? (*Sleep; socially; time outdoors; hobbies; exercise; work.*)

....

....

....

....

....

6. Schedule in spontaneity

Can you remember the last time you enjoyed a meal out with friends that hadn't been marked on your calendar weeks, or even months, in advance? Or recall a day when you ignored your to-do list and acted on the spur of the moment, simply because the sun was shining brightly and spending a couple of hours in the park with a book seemed a better idea than being stuck indoors? Altering your routine, even now and again, can be empowering. Do it spontaneously, without great thought or planning, and a break from the norm will add excitement and richness to what was originally destined to be the "same old, same old" day.

On your daily bus journey, do you always sit on the same seat on the left? Look at the same view out of the window? Next time, choose a seat on the right and see the world from a different angle. What do you see?

....

....

....

....

....

....

....

....

Does lunch usually involve a quick sandwich on the go or at your desk? If the weather allows, eat outside. Don't plan a route. Just walk 10 minutes in one direction. Where do you end up?

....

....

....

....

....

....

....

....

Is your talk sweet enough?

Throughout the day, the mind keeps up an incessant commentary of what you're doing. It's called "self-talk." Sometimes it's encouraging but more often than not it can be negative and critical. Here's how to change the language of your inner dialogue.

Ever think you're the only one who talks to themselves? You're not alone, everyone has a voice chattering inside their head, giving approval and dishing out criticism. And it matters, because you're the one listening to it.

Think for a moment about the occasions you talk to yourself. Perhaps it's when you're about to go out the door and you glance at yourself in the mirror; when you're feeling excited or unsure about something; when you make a mistake or do something right. By paying attention, you become more aware of the inner dialogue and the messages you're giving yourself.

What tone does your inner voice use most often? Is it friendly and encouraging, celebrating the big and small wins in your day? Or is your inner voice your inner critic, making harsh comments? Too often you speak to yourself with words you would never say to a friend, often without even realizing it.

Your inner critic

Your inner critic applies a strange kind of logic, a protective layer of sorts. If you think the worst of yourself first, you can't be hurt if someone else criticizes you, because you've already heard it.

You may think that there are benefits to having an inner critic. Sometimes you need a little verbal elbow in the ribs to move you forward or strengthen your decision. But this is better coming from the encouraging voice of a cheerleader rather than the sniping of an inner critic.

Does it matter if your inner critic is being unkind or hurtful? What is the benefit of being told you're stupid, that you look like a mess, or you're bad at something? When what you say to yourself makes you feel bad, your inner voice is serving no helpful purpose.

No name calling

How your inner critic phrases its comments plays a big part in how the words affect you. Speaking in absolute terms can be damning.

For example, if you send an email to the wrong person you might tell yourself "I'm such an idiot" rather than "it was a mistake not to double check the email before sending." The first statement labels you as an idiot while the second is more accurate—you made a mistake. It doesn't define you as an idiotic person. The difference between the two statements may appear subtle, but the message you're giving yourself is quite different.

By paying attention to your self-talk, you can change the message and how you say it. Your inner voice is yours and you can exert your control over it. Use it not as a critic but as a motivator. Be your own best friend. The more kind and encouraging you are to yourself, the more able you will be to express the same positivity to others.

Choose your words wisely

How often do you use these words to start a sentence?

I should, I have to, I need to, I've got to...

A few times a day? Does it matter? Well, they all have something in common—a sense of obligation, a lack of choice. By starting a sentence with "I have to" you're saying that you're obliged to do whatever follows, you've little choice in the matter. There are times when this is true: you may need to leave home at a certain time to be at a specific appointment. There are occasions when there is a clear obligation but using the words "should," "have to," or "need" can give the task a negative tone.

Let's say you have to pick up your children from school. Technically you're right—it's your responsibility. But "have to" has an underlying tone of duty, it's a more negative than positive sentiment. Begin the sentence with "I'm going to" or "I will be" and it becomes more neutrally factual. If you're already feeling the pressure of a busy day, saying that you *have* to do something, whether it's to yourself or another person, will compound the feeling of stress.

Imagine reading a to-do list. If the list reads: "I'm going to... then I'll... next I will..." it feels achievable. If instead you read the list as: "I have to... then I need to... next I've got to..." you can feel the mounting pressure of the tasks increasing with each one. The to-do list or your responsibilities aren't changed by the language you use, but it does change your mindset and attitude toward them.

There are times when these obligatory-sounding words aren't really appropriate in the context you use them. For example, you could say you need to tidy the kitchen before going to bed. Is this really necessary? What are the consequences if you don't? In reality would you just prefer it if you went to bed knowing the kitchen is no longer messy? In which case what you mean to say is that you want an organized kitchen before you go to bed so you're going to tidy it. The task has become a choice.

Focusing on language in this way may seem like semantics but these seemingly subtle differences have an impact on your state of mind, how you see yourself and what you do. By being more aware of your language and choosing words that more accurately match your actions, you can begin to create a more positive mindset for yourself.

"Be kinder to yourself. And then let your kindness flood the world."
Pema Chödrön

Listen to yourself

- Be mindful of how you speak to yourself and what you say
- If it's a positive message, give it your attention and believe it
- If it's critical, challenge yourself for evidence of the criticism
- If it's exaggerating, check if you're talking in absolutes or specifics
- Apply the no name-calling rule
- Be mindful of how often you say "*I have to...,*" "*I need to...,*" and "*I should...*"
- Replace them with neutral words such as "*I'm going to...*" or "*I will...,*" or a positive start such as "*I'm looking forward to...*"

This exercise can help to reframe observations made by your inner critic in a friendly, positive way.

Get into a habit of listening to your inner voice. The more you can tune in to what it is saying, the quicker you will begin to notice when it turns negative—thoughts like "*I can't do it,*" "*I'm not good enough,*" "*I'm bad at...,*" "*I'll never be able to...*" Record any negative self-talk here, alongside where and when it happens.

....

....

....

....

....

Now speak more positively. Talk to yourself like you would a child, with love and care. Ask things like: "*What would I say to a friend in a similar situation?*" or "*Is there anything that will help me to do this?*" and swap negatives for motivational phrases like: "*Come on!*" and "*You can do this!*" Record your positive mantras here.

....

....

....

....

....

....

little
things
make
big
days

Take a joy ride

Many people have blocked the path to letting themselves feel joy. Here's how to bring it back into your life and keep it flowing.

There can be many times in your life when you feel happy: giving or receiving a thoughtful birthday present, passing an exam, even finding a seat on a packed commuter train. It tends to be fleeting. Joy, however, can be elusive, even though it comes from deep within your heart and everyone is capable of experiencing it.

What is joy and how do you access it?

"I'd define joy as a source. If happiness is the water, joy is the fountain," says mindset and leadership coach Emma Tynan. "It's accessed through doing and experiencing things that make you feel good." According to Emma, everyone has a deep source of joy within them, but they seldom access it even though it should be a priority. "Joy is waiting to be experienced through you. But so many of us put it on the back-burner in our lives," she explains. "We stand in our own way. We deny, put off, don't spend or cancel doing things that will bring us joy. Allowing yourself to experience joy is a profound act of self-love and your own responsibility."

Learn to love yourself

Personal and professional development consultant Mary Hykel Hunt says that deeply held beliefs and influences from childhood can hold people back from experiencing a more joyful way of being. Sometimes self-love and self-care, the very things that can open up a more joyful life, take the lowest priority on their to-do lists. Other people's needs often take priority ahead of their own, something that frequently originates from their formative years. "We can block ourselves through our own homegrown belief sets—what we really believe is possible, deep down. These beliefs are seeded in childhood and, if they tend to be of a negative hue, they can block our ability to change," she says.

This unconscious blocking of the "good things" can be released, and it's all down to how much you value yourself. "Absolutely nothing is being withheld from you, only you do that with how worthy you feel," says Emma. "You will always receive what you believe you are worthy of."

Become aware of negative self-beliefs

Tune in to what's going on in your subconscious mind. Start to notice any negative thoughts and feelings you have or self-destructive behavior you exhibit and note the consequences. These are most likely to become apparent when you feel yourself resisting something.

Keep a note of what comes to mind here in this journal. Writing down your thoughts is a powerful tool that provides you with greater insight and self-knowledge. By keeping a record you will start to easily recognize any self-sabotage patterns that emerge. Underlying these will be the limiting beliefs you have formed. Their root source may be the result of your reactions to past experiences, feedback from others, or perhaps even the culture in which you grew up. Try to identify what they are.

What do you believe about yourself and your abilities? Are they valid? What would your friends or family think of them?

....

....

....

....

....

....

....

....

....

....

....

....

....

....

....

....

Tap into your own joy

Joy is personal. Once you realize what it is that brings you joy, you are more able to make the most of the opportunities that are already present in your life. Tynan recommends beginning with one simple, regular action to create joy in your life:

Ask yourself this question in your meditation practice or while you're having a quiet time in the morning: "What will bring me joy today?" Then do it!

Allowing yourself to have or do the things that you constantly put off, or dismiss, for whatever reason, is the key to making your life more joyful. "Invest in that yoga retreat, get the massage, treat yourself to a beautiful meal, do the flower-arranging course, take the ceramics class, walk on the beach with your dog. Whatever is calling you is an opportunity to tap into your joy," advises Tynan. Do more of whatever brings you joy. It's a simple gift that you can give yourself, and the people around you naturally benefit too.

List three things here that would bring you joy.

➤ ....
....
....
➤ ....
....
....
➤ ....
....
....

"One of the secrets of a happy life is continuous small treats."

Iris Murdoch

From joy to gratitude

Another simple act can transform your life into one where joy has a prominent place—gratitude. "When we're discontented or unhappy, we tend to walk around in a fog of dissatisfaction, repeating to ourselves time-worn mantras that usually start with if only...; if only I had more money...; if only I could find my soul-mate...; if only I could find another job...; if only I could sell my house...," says personal development consultant Mary Hykel Hunt. "Cultivating an attitude of gratitude is a major fuel source. This isn't just about being grateful for what you're going to get—it's more about being grateful for what you already have. Gratitude is like a magnet. It attracts more of the things or feelings that you're grateful for."

Allowing joy to manifest in your life also means believing it is feasible and you are capable of creating it. "Just wishing or hoping for something is not enough, if it comes into conflict with what we believe is possible," says Mary. "If I'm asking for something I don't really think is possible, it's unlikely to happen because I'll miss the cues that would help usher it in, or I'll be unable to think openly enough to keep the door open for miracles to enter. We need to dig down and find out what we believe is possible." It's simple—identify what brings you joy, allow yourself to do more of it, and experience the joyful life you deserve.

List five small things and acts for which you feel grateful today.

➤ ....

....

➤ ....

....

➤ ....

....

➤ ....

....

➤ ....

....

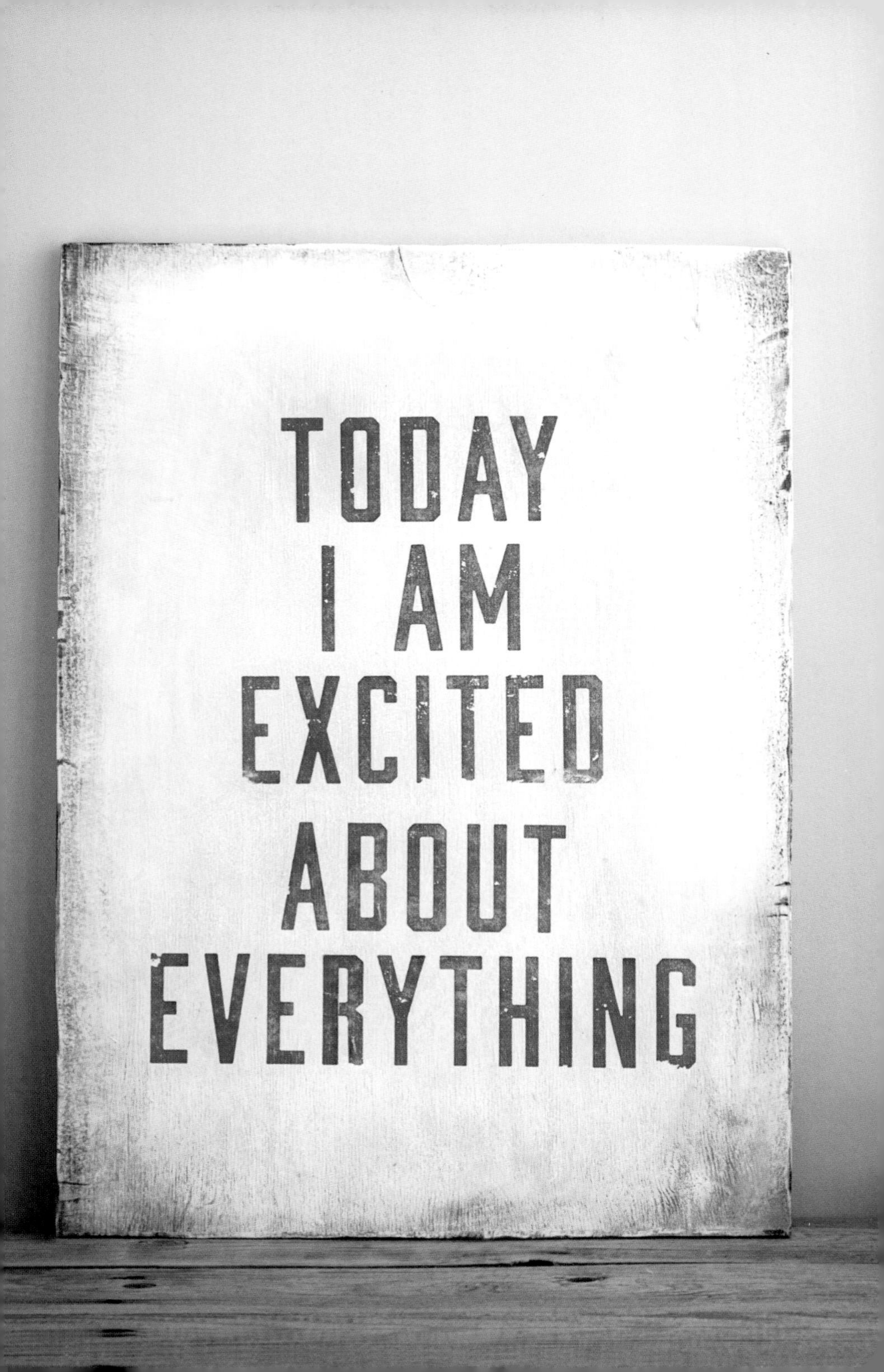
TODAY
I AM
EXCITED
ABOUT
EVERYTHING

You are how you eat

It's time to slow down, avoid distractions, and focus on the manner in which you consume your food.

When you have limited time it's easy to find yourself eating on the go or at your desk, multitasking while you munch. This often leads to a quick refuel where you choose food you'd normally avoid and then scoff too much of it, too quickly. Have you ever opened a packet of cookies while busy, with the intention of just having a couple? With your mind distracted, your hand automatically reaches for one cookie after another and the next time you look the packet's empty. What's more, you have little recollection of polishing them off—let alone how they tasted.

Mindful eating is about being aware of what—and how much—you're consuming. It's so easy to dig into a meal without thinking and in the process undo any good intentions you have about eating the right kind of food, at the right time, in the right quantity.

There are two stages to eating mindfully: planning the food you intend to put on your plate and being aware while you are eating it.

STAGE 1
Planning your meals

- It takes the stress out of deciding what to have each day because you've already been through the process

- It saves money because you only buy what you plan to eat

- It saves time because you go to the shops (or click online) with a list rather than wandering the aisles hoping for inspiration

- You throw away less food as you're buying planned meals

- You can make sure you're getting food you really like, and that it ticks your own healthy, nutritious boxes

- It makes it less likely that you'll miss out on meals or spontaneously buy unhealthy snacks to plug a hunger pang

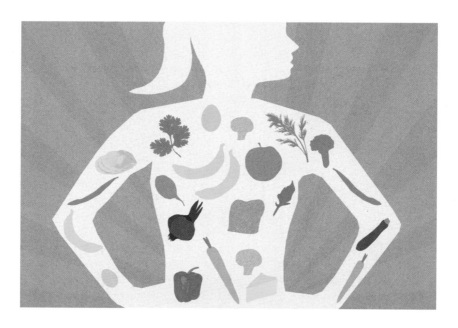

STAGE 2
Being more aware

If you're having lunch while typing, ironing, or taking a call you can get to the end of the meal and have no recollection of what you've just eaten. The sensory experience has been lost because your attention was elsewhere.

When you have no distractions, and you're able to focus on the food in front of you and the action of eating, you're more aware of how appetizing it looks, the smells, textures, and tastes.

Giving the food in front of you your full attention for the few minutes it takes to eat it can be enormously beneficial. You will:

- Notice its appearance
- Feel its heat or coolness, and its textures on your tongue
- Inhale its aroma
- Really taste it, perhaps identifying ingredients, herbs, or spices
- Realize when you're full because you've paid attention to what and how much you've eaten, and eaten more slowly

The last point is an important one. If you were to sit with a box of chocolates in front of you and focus only on each chocolate as you ate it, it's unlikely you'd have as many as you would if your mind were preoccupied with other thoughts.

Mindful eating meditation

This isn't a recipe for how to eat all your meals. It's a way of increasing your appreciation of the food you consume and bringing your focus to the present moment. By doing this, you give your whirring mind a break and replace it with a few minutes of calm. This example uses a piece of chocolate, but choose whichever food you prefer.

- Remove yourself from anything that could distract your attention for the next few minutes.
- Sit down with a piece of chocolate on a plate in front of you.
- Notice the shape, color, texture, and markings on the chocolate.
- Lean in and inhale the cocoa aroma. How does the smell make you feel?
- Think about the journey the chocolate has taken to reach your plate— the cocoa beans growing, being harvested, processed, packaged, and the distances they've traveled to arrive here in front of you.
- Pick up the square of chocolate, how does it feel in your fingers? Soft, hard, light, heavy?
- Place it in your mouth and just hold it there for a moment, without chewing or swallowing, noticing the sensation on your tongue.
- Begin to chew slowly, focusing your attention on the flavor, its intensity. Is it sweet or bitter?
- If you want to swallow it, notice that feeling first and stay with it as long as possible.
- Then, as you swallow the chocolate slowly, follow the sensation as it travels down your throat to your stomach.
- Enjoy any lingering textures or flavors. Savor the moment.

Weekly meal plan

Getting into the habit of creating a meal plan for the week ahead makes writing shopping lists really simple. Use the space below to start.

Monday

....

....

....

Tuesday

....

....

....

Wednesday

....

....

....

Thursday

....

....

....

Friday

....

....

....

Saturday

....

....

....

Sunday

....

....

....

NOTES

Born to be wild

As modern life puts up more barriers to the natural world, many people feel something important is being lost from their lives and are looking to reengage with nature. This needn't mean quitting work and moving into a tepee in the woods—whether you live in a city apartment or a house in the suburbs, there are simple ways to achieve your own personal "rewilding" and restore that connection.

Few people have ever lived in a truly wild place. Modern life intrudes into almost every location on Earth. In the US, around 80 percent of the population live in urban environments surrounded by concrete, steel, and plastic where often the only wildlife is a local fox. Everything around us, from the possessions we accumulate to the house where we live, takes us farther away from the natural world. But there is no evidence it makes people happy. In fact, research suggests the opposite. A 2013 study of 10,000 people by Exeter University in the UK found those living near green spaces reported greater well-being than those for whom parkland was limited.

This could explain why increasing numbers of people are learning to "rewild." Traditionally, the term was used in conservation to describe the removal of man-made barriers and allow animals to roam freely. Recently, however, it's also been used to describe a process of people choosing to reengage with nature. And while the word might conjure up images of survival training or isolation in the wilderness it is, in fact, a simple practice anyone can try. It could involve meditating in nature, for example, or studying plant medicine, or spending a night in a wild place. The goal is to open your heart to the natural world and connect to the wildness within.

"Just living is not enough. One must have sunshine, freedom, and a little flower."

Hans Christian Andersen

Nurture your connection

Kevin Park and his partner Alissa Wild founded We Are Wildness in 2011 from their home on Vancouver Island. It began as a Facebook page but has evolved into an online community of 350,000 people. Via their website, it is possible to study anything from natural movement to tracking wildlife. It also offers the opportunity to participate in the Rewild Your Life Thirty-Day Challenge, a course that inspires people to get outdoors for 30 minutes every day for 30 days. In 2016, Gwynneth Hamann researched the effects of the challenge and found that people who participated showed "significant increases in mood, well-being, mindfulness, and meaning."

Park points out that people's physical bodies can benefit too. "Most things in the modern lifestyle weaken immune systems and harm health, like late nights, stress, poor diet, poor air quality, too much exposure to magnetic fields, and electronic devices... the list goes on. Focusing on adding things into your life that build your physical health leaves less room for the things that harm it."

He believes that rewilding also has psychological benefits. "Any time you allow more nature and natural practices into your life your mental health can improve. Who doesn't feel uplifted after a walk in the woods or a visit to the ocean?" Official research supports his views. In 2015, Stanford University found that people who walked in nature showed decreased activity in the part of the brain associated with depression.

Kenton Whitman from Wisconsin runs ReWild University. He mentors people as they spend time in the wild and urges them to remember their ancestors' traits, such as curiosity and passion. "Rewilding taps into something you already possess," he says, ". . . a vibrant, wise inner-nature that will guide you better than any book or course. Believing in that inner nature and taking small steps to tap into it, then paying attention to what happens, that's all it takes to get started."

Four ways to rewild yourself

1. Pick one thing

Focus on something that you see every day: a tree, squirrel, flower, or bird. Note how it transforms as time passes.

2. Draw nature

Birds, leaves, stones, flowers, bark. Fill these pages with your sketches.

3. Step outside

Look around you. Notice nature in your surroundings. Do trees line the road?
Are there clouds in the sky? What is moving—birds flying overhead, leaves in the
wind, insects buzzing?

4. Walk in the park

Notice the texture of the grass and soil, the smells and the colors. If there are flowers, observe the stage of their growth. Have the buds fully opened? Focus on physical sensations. What do you see, feel, and hear?

Mindful photography

Creativity can be stifled by negative self-talk and anxiety. But with a little practice you can learn to adopt a beginner's mind, trust your instincts, and let go of your expectations—then you can stop looking and start seeing.

Humans are a funny lot. From the moment they wake up in the morning they're in a rush to complete everything on their to-do list before their head hits the pillow at night. They pride themselves on their ability to multitask: texting people while standing in line at the supermarket, listening to music while driving, checking social media while eating. They measure the success of their day by how much they can cram into it. As they tackle each job, a voice shouts inside their head criticizing, or occasionally praising, their every move.

Imagine you're standing in the supermarket line when you become aware of a rack of candy bars nearby. And the inner dialogue begins: "They look good; I shouldn't have one, but I've had a tough day. I can't believe what happened in the meeting. That guy's got it in for me. Maybe I should look for another job. I don't want to let everybody down." And so on.

But what has this to do with photography?

Well, when your mind is preoccupied with thoughts about the past, or concerns about the future, you lose your connection with the present. If you stand before a mountain with your and ready to go but your mind is distracted, there is no limit to the one-sided conversation you can have with yourself. This self-talk can be destructive and takes up headspace that could be used for creative thoughts.

How can you silence this inner critic?

You can't, not entirely anyway. What you can do is turn down the volume.
Let's return to the mountain for a minute. You've been standing there for a while,
your feet are getting cold, and your mind is wandering. The diatribe is in full
flow: "I haven't taken anything good yet. I need to go home with a few good shots
or the day will have been wasted." You get the idea.

When your mind drifts off like this, you have lost touch with your
surroundings: the mountain, the clouds, the play of light on the peak. Your
concentration has disappeared, and any moments of pure observation are
virtually impossible.

Now you need to bring yourself back to the present...

To do this, you have to recognize when your inner critic turns up and roll out the
welcome mat. If you try to stop the flow of thoughts they will multiply, causing
you more trouble. Your mind will go into overdrive: "Why can't I stop thinking?
Surely no one else struggles like this. I must be doing it wrong."

As soon as you welcome the thoughts, you can start work. Your first job is to
notice any emotions you attach to the thoughts. When you are waiting for the
"right" light, for example, do you feel impatient, happy, or bored? Your inner voice
is so keen to label every experience as either good or bad, worthy or wasteful, it's
hard to stay neutral. Having noticed these emotions, you need to practice letting
go of them, without trying to change them or cling to them.

If your feet are cold, for example, you just say to yourself "discomfort" and
let the feeling pass. If you haven't taken a good picture all day, you just say
"disappointment" and let it pass. With practice, the number of thoughts and
emotions should decrease, which allows creativity and fresh insights to float
to the surface.

"These mountains that you are carrying, you were only supposed to climb."
Najwa Zebian

What is your self-talk right now?

....

....

....

....

....

....

....

....

....

....

....

....

What emotions do you attach to these thoughts? Can you assign a single word to each emotion, and let it go?

....

....

....

....

....

....

....

....

....

....

....

....

Three exercises to help open your eyes—and your mind

EXERCISE 1

Understanding light and emotions

Every photographer is aware that light plays a significant role, but how often do you notice—really notice—how it affects your mood, and the artistic decisions you make? Imagine you've traveled some distance to reach a location, for example. You've set up your gear in plenty of time, but the light you envisioned simply hasn't materialized. How do you react? Do you feel agitated, causing you to pack up your gear and head for home, or do you see the unexpected conditions as an opportunity to try something new? Are you able to remain receptive and open to new ways of seeing?

Record your thoughts here.

....

....

....

To acknowledge the connection between light and emotions, consider the following before releasing the shutter: Where is the light coming from? Is it hard or soft, warm or cold, bright or dim? Is the contrast high or low? How does each of these properties make you feel? Maybe the light is so warm that it reminds you of a relaxing family vacation, how does this association affect your current decision-making and, in turn, your photography? Do you favor one kind of light over another? Does this bias lead to missed opportunities? Take time out to make the connection.

Warm light makes me feel...

....

....

Cold light makes me feel...

....

....

EXERCISE 2

Appreciating the interconnectedness of objects

Photographers isolate a moment in time. On some occasions they use large apertures to isolate subjects from their natural surroundings. More often than not they work alone, having chosen to isolate themselves from others. In fact, if you think about it, photography and isolation are strongly linked. But what if you turn things on their head and consider each subject as connected to the rest of the world, interdependent even. How does this affect your approach?

Take a tree, for example. Find a spot in front of an established one and sit at its base. Soften your gaze and rest it on a section of the trunk. Now consider all of the forces that come together to support its very existence: the roots that absorb moisture and dissolved minerals from the soil, the trunk that supports limbs while transporting nutrients from roots to leaves, the bark that protects it from external attack, and the buds that eventually develop into leaves. Think about the sunlight the tree needs to trigger photosynthesis, the rain it requires for moisture, and the wind that disperses its seeds. In reality, nothing is truly isolated.

Look around you. What do you notice? Is there an object you could focus on to practice this exercise?

....

....

....

....

....

....

....

....

....

....

....

....

EXERCISE 3

Moving beyond boredom

The late Diane Arbus was responsible for this wonderful photographic quote:

"The Chinese have a theory that you pass through boredom into fascination and I think it's true."

At some point everyone is guilty of taking the easy option, namely shooting a subject whose beauty is so instant and obvious that it leads to predictable pictures. One way of passing through boredom is to take an everyday object and explore it more fully. Choose something that, in your opinion, has no aesthetic value: a toothbrush, coffee cup, or cheese grater, for example. Look about you. What can you see?

For the next few minutes keep your camera close by, but switched off. Now give your full attention to the subject you have chosen, noticing texture, lines, patterns, forms, shapes, and shadows, and how they relate to each other. View it from every angle—trace its contours with your fingers and use a mirror to obtain fresh viewpoints. Now, without trying to create a good photograph, pick up your camera and start shooting. Repeat the exercise with a stretch of sidewalk, or even a patch of flooring. The results can be fascinating.

As you experiment with the previous exercises, fill these pages with your photographs. It will help you to recall the feelings you had as you took them every time you look back through this journal.

I dreamed a dream

When you dream, the brain bursts into life, creating a mysterious alternate reality. But scientists are no closer to agreeing why it does this than they were when it was still regarded as divine intervention. What do your dreams mean to you?

A dream job, I must be dreaming, a dreamy day... the word "dream" has a curious number of applications. It is a nighttime vision that might be good or bad; it is an aspiration of something earnestly sought but unlikely to be achieved; it is something singularly lovely and without blemish. All of them denote something that is otherworldly in nature. In the hands of psychoanalyst Sigmund Freud, however, dreams were "the royal road to the unconscious" and thus the mind itself.

What happens when you dream

Everyone dreams, even those who insist they don't. They just can't remember them. The average night's sleep is described in terms of a cycle. It consists of five distinct stages but it is only during the final stage—REM (rapid eye movement) sleep—that people experience the most vivid and memorable dreams. The body is in a strange hinterland at this point. The breathing becomes shallow and irregular, limb muscles are temporarily paralyzed, and the eyes begin to flicker. The brain goes to great lengths to preserve this dream state, and external sounds like alarm clocks are often incorporated into the dream narrative, so as not to interrupt the flow.

No two people dream alike: a dream can last for a few seconds or nearly half an hour, with longer dreams occurring later on in the sleep cycle. Most people have between three or five dreams a night and unless you write down what you have dreamed as soon as you wake up, you are likely to forget it. Tests have shown that the brain is as active during REM sleep as if it was awake, but what is it doing?

William Dement is a pioneering sleep researcher and founder of the Sleep Research Center at Stanford University. He found that subjects who were deep in REM sleep demonstrated high levels of tension, anxiety, and irritability, plus a lack of coordination and an inability to concentrate when they were woken up. His conclusion was that dreaming was vital to cognitive health and well-being, even if he could not establish exactly how.

Why dreams are important

David Billington is the research development officer at the Dream Research Institute in London, which is studying the therapeutic effects of dreams and has undertaken a number of studies to establish whether dreams are good for health. In a pilot study of a group who recorded their dreams on a regular basis, there was a measurable increase in personal well-being.

David recommends the practice of keeping a dream journal. He believes that recorded recollections can be a powerful aid to self-healing: "It can help people to see their life in a slightly different way. It says something about who we are and what we are and serves as an affirmation or something new, which can be fascinating."

When it comes to what you should write, he has this advice: "It's just a question of recall. Even the slightest fragment, write it down. It may be a color, or a feeling, or the vaguest image, just scribbling something down will help you to be more specific. If you do keep at it, you can reflect on the themes that are coming through."

And for those who may be troubled by recurring dreams, David has reassuring words: "It is a problem only if someone perceives it as a problem. If it's not disruptive but is merely curious it could just be that something in the unconscious wants to be known. Sometimes it can be something we don't want to deal with and this becomes expressed as a dream experience."

"Dreams, if they're any good, are always a little bit crazy."
Ray Charles

Keep a dream diary

Getting into a habit of recalling your dreams on a regular basis can help you to remember them more clearly. Try recording them for a week in this journal.

- Keep a pen and paper beside your bed. Start recording your dream as soon as you wake up.

- Before writing, quickly rewind the dream in your mind, to make sure you can recall the narrative from beginning to end, otherwise you may start to forget it as you write.

- Note any scenery or objects, the setting, prevailing atmosphere, and the people present. Some things that may not appear relevant could be there for a reason so don't leave anything out, however bizarre.

- Look for any reappearance of events or situations from the day before. This "day residue" could be important if the subconscious is trying to link it to other memories.

- How did the dream make you feel? Record your mood when you wake up. The emotions you experience in a dream can be telling. If you wake up worried or relieved, ask yourself why. With practice you may find your dreams offer some insight into your subconscious.

"Why does the eye see a thing more clearly in dreams than the imagination when awake?"

Leonardo da Vinci

Monday

....

Tuesday

Thursday

Friday

....

Saturday

Sunday

Open book

Few pleasures in life are as simple and enjoyable as curling up with a good book, and with a little mindfulness, time spent reading can become an even more rewarding experience.

A rainy Sunday afternoon with a hot drink, a comfy couch, and a book to read for a couple of hours—nothing could be nicer. Or could it? It's all too easy to get stuck, reading the same page over and over again. You realize the words aren't sinking in, and you feel the need to wade through prose you're simply not enjoying. So how can you truly savor the precious time you spend reading?

Find your space

Taking time to employ a little mindfulness can get you in the right frame of mind to properly sink into a book.

- Try to clear your space and mind of any distractions.
- Turn your phone to silent or, better still, switch it off.
- Find a quiet space where you can be alone or, if it helps, have soft music playing in the background.
- The bath is a popular place to read because it's free of distractions, and the relaxing warmth and pleasant scent as you soak can also help to clear your mind.
- If your head is buzzing with thoughts and things you have to do, get them done first.
- If they're time-consuming or complicated, jot them down so they form an external list.
- Now, prepare to sink into the world of your book. Don't underestimate the pleasure and anticipation that can be found in purely holding it, feeling the texture of the cover, slowly turning the pages, and breathing in its smell.

Take the book in your hands. How does it feel? Heavy or light? Rough or smooth?

....

....

....

What does the cover illustration make you think of?

....

....

....

How does the title sound?

....

....

....

....

Choosing well

There is much joy to be found in surrounding yourself with books, stacking them in piles around the house, but choosing ones that will bring you genuine pleasure isn't straightforward. Don't pick up a book because you feel it's one you ought to have read or because everyone else is raving about it. Also, don't dismiss a book simply because you've read it before. Rereading a well-loved volume can be like meeting an old friend.

There's a lot of pleasure to be found in visiting a bookstore or library and browsing. Look for titles that appeal, covers that please, and synopses that intrigue, and don't forget to check for reviews by other library-goers or bookstore assistants. It's a great way to discover unbiased, genuine opinions.

Bestseller lists can be helpful, but just because everybody else has loved a book doesn't mean you will. Similarly, awards are a good indicator of quality, but the theme might not be one you enjoy or you may dislike the style of prose.

Use this exercise to help work out your tastes and preferences.

List five, or 10 at most, of your all-time favorite books. Now study your list
and see if you can spot any common threads. Are they all historical romances?
Do they have a magical element? Is there a character trait in the lead protagonist
that intrigues you? If you can find a link, you'll know what to look for when
scouting for your next read.

All-time favorites

Book title ....

Theme ....

....

....

Book title ....

Theme ....

....

....

Book title ....

Theme ....

....

....

Book title ....

Theme ....

....

....

Book title ....

Theme ....

....

....

Book title ....

Theme ....

....

....

Book title ....

Theme ....

....

....

Book title ....

Theme ....

....

....

Book title ....

Theme ....

....

....

Book title ....

Theme ....

....

....

Wonderful words

With a bit of luck the previous exercise will lead you to one of those books where an author makes a comment that feels as if it has been plucked out of your own mind. When you discover these books, savor them and remember them.

Use the space below to record favorite lines or passages that find a place in your heart.

This meditative exercise should take 15 to 20 minutes, so make yourself comfortable in a room where you won't be disturbed. Lie on your back on a mat or rug on the floor, or on your bed. You might want to cover yourself with a blanket and rest your head on a cushion or pillow.

Mindful body scan

Use this simple exercise to help create a healthy relationship with your body.

1   Slowly let your eyes close and take a few moments to get in touch with the sensations of your body. Listen to your breathing and feel the places where your body makes contact with the floor or the bed. On every out-breath, allow yourself to gently let go, slowly sinking a little deeper into the mat or bed.

2   Starting with your head, focus on this area, feeling its weight as it rests on the cushion. Now introduce your forehead, noticing whether or not you can feel any stress or tension. Then include your eyes, nose, cheeks, mouth, chin, and finally ears, including any sounds you might be able to hear. Be aware, moment by moment, of the changing pattern of sensations in your body and your breathing. If you notice your mind wandering, acknowledge it, and then gently guide your mind back to the part of the body you are focusing on.

3   Slowly release the focus on your head and face, and move your awareness to your neck and shoulders, being conscious of your breathing at all times. Notice the strong muscles in this part of the body and be aware of any tension or tightness in this area, which is common. If you find any tension, breathe into it on the in-breath and let go of it on the out-breath, releasing the sensation from your body. Extend your awareness into your arms, elbows, wrists, hands, and fingers, and focus on your breathing.

4   Shift your focus to your chest, noticing the sensation of the subtle rise and fall with each in-breath and out-breath. If you notice any tension, or aches and pains, breathe into them and out again, releasing them from your body.

5   Concentrate on the physical sensations in the lower abdomen and any changes you feel as you slowly breathe in and out—it may help you to put your hands on your belly to really feel each breath. Extend your awareness to your lower back, feeling the gentle pressure as it touches the floor.

6   Bring your focus down to your legs. Feel the weight from the tops of your thighs, right down to your ankles, gently notice what sensations are here, such as the way they rest on the floor, or whether there is any numbness or tingling.

7   Move your attention into both of your feet, focusing on the soles, the heels, the upper part, and finally your toes, concentrating on each one in turn—the big toe, the little toe, and the ones in between. When you are ready, breathe in and gently feel the sensation of your breath as it moves down your body and into your toes; then, on the out-breath, feel it coming back up again, releasing any tension or discomfort. Continue for a few breaths.

8   Take one or two deeper breaths in and out, filling your whole body, then spend a few more minutes lying on the floor. Relax, breathing freely.

The art of travel

The daily commute leaves many people drained before they've even arrived at work and stressed out when they return home. Practicing mindfulness during the journey can set you up for a better day and a more rewarding evening.

Most people find the daily commute to work stressful—whether stuck in traffic on a muggy morning or fighting their way on to a crowded late bus home, only to be faced with the choice of sitting next to an angry man loudly venting his frustration or a woman coughing feverishly. The hours spent getting to and from work can often seem like time wasted and leave you feeling depleted before you've even started.

Increasingly, however, commuters are using this seemingly lost time to their advantage, practicing mindful techniques on crowded trains and among honking horns to bring a sense of well-being that will help them accept the journey's inevitable chaos and better prepare them for the day.

Adopting a more peaceful and thoughtful mindset while traveling to and from work can only be a good thing. Mindful commuters report feeling less stressed, arriving at work with a more positive outlook that helps them get the best from their day. It stands to reason that if you've spent your journey to work fretting about being late, or angry that a fellow traveler took the last seat, you'll arrive agitated and in a negative frame of mind. This, in turn, can set the tone of your day, weaving its way through your emotions, informing decisions, and coloring your attitude toward colleagues. Similarly, they return home able to be more present and aware of their environment.

"Everything we see depends on how we look at it."

Katrina Mayer

Changing your mindset

Noticing how you are making physical contact with the world is a good place to start. Whether it's your feet in touch with the ground or the pedals of a bicycle, or your hands on the steering wheel, having a sense of physical engagement with your surroundings helps to bring the mind to focus and root you to your environment. Really observing the world around you—how a tree changes with the seasons, the luminous shade of a certain door, the pattern of cracks in the sidewalk—will neutralize negative thoughts by occupying your mind with snippets of the here and now.

Paying attention to your breathing is another stress-relieving technique that can easily be adopted while traveling and deliver a sense of space and well-being among the crowds and hustle. Focusing the mind on the gentle in and out of your breaths helps to calm the body and diffuse anxiety. It centers you on the moment and draws attention away from potential stressful incidents. It isn't going to make those situations go away, but it helps you to deal with them in a calmer, more considerate manner.

Although difficult, learning to see negatives as positives really changes your attitude toward your commute. Standing in line infuriates most people, but try seeing it as an excuse to rest and observe the world: people-watching is a wonderful pastime and can counteract feelings of impatience. Not getting on a bus or a train because it's overcrowded means it's more likely the next one will have space. The roadworks that are currently adding 20 minutes to your journey will save you 10 minutes when they're finished. Positive thinking opens the mind, encourages you to be more empathetic, and allows you to be more creative.

"The world is a book and those who do not travel read only one page."

Saint Augustine

Ways to bring mindfulness
to your journey

- Leave in plenty of time. Rushing and fretting about being late is certain to cause anxiety and stress. If you arrive early, make the most of it to rest and clear your mind before you start.

- Don't fill your journey with technology. Phones and tablets are an easy way to pass the time, but they generally add to a sense of mind clutter. Keep them in your pocket or bag and instead observe the world around you and your place in it.

- If it's possible, take a different route. Seeing the same things every day can add to your feeling of being on autopilot. A change of scenery means you get to see new things that help to develop your sense of curiosity and creativity.

- Walk wherever possible. The slower pace and change of perspective will help to calm and settle your mind. Even if this means getting off the bus or subway a couple of stops early, the benefits are worth it.

- Pay attention to your breathing. Focusing on the breath will help with all aspects of mindfulness.

- Engage with the physical world. Bring your attention to how your feet make contact with the ground, or how the wind feels in your face.

- Use the movement and rhythm of the train or bus to help you get into a more peaceful state of mind.

- Notice your body and how it is responding. Are your shoulders rigid? Are you holding your breath? Is your neck tight? Quietly bring your attention to areas that need relaxing and focus on reducing tension.

- Try to see negatives as positives. To begin with, treat it as an exercise—when you notice yourself taking a pessimistic attitude, think of its opposite. In time, this will develop into a habit and start to become more intuitive.

- Embrace the journey and make friends with your commute. For most people it's an unavoidable aspect of life. In reclaiming the time and using it to be more mindful, you enrich yourself and become better equipped to deal with the challenges of the day.

Moving meditation

Next time you're traveling by bus or train, use the journey as an opportunity to engage your senses and observe the world around you.

SEE

Look around you, at everything. Notice any people sitting or standing nearby. Are they happy, or sad? Are they traveling alone, or with others? Look closely at the inside of the carriage or vehicle. Is it clean? What colors or marks can you see?

FEEL

Think about how your body feels. Notice the vibrations in your feet as the train or bus moves along. If you're standing, focus on how your body is keeping balance. Gently shift your weight from side to side. Feel the muscles working in your thighs, knees, and ankles. If you're sitting, is the seat hard or soft?

HEAR

Are people around you talking? Let their chatter wash over you. Maybe the doors are opening or closing. Listen to the sounds of the engine, wheels, or tracks. Focus on the rhythm and try to feel any changes—are you going faster or slowing down?

SMELL

Close your eyes and take a deep breath in through your nose. Buses and trains often have distinctive metallic smells—notice them. Is there a faint smell of exhaust? Something musty or damp?

Open your eyes and look outside. Relax and listen out for your stop.

Each day this week, imagine it's the first time you've been on this journey. Make notes and draw sketches of the things you see and feel—the coolness of the air entering your lungs, the beauty of a tree as you pass by.

Monday

....

Tuesday

Wednesday

Thursday

Friday

NOTES

Reasons to be cheerful

Writing a gratitude journal is a simple and increasingly popular way of boosting happiness.

Psychologists have discovered that regularly practicing gratitude can have a measurably positive effect on well-being. Work undertaken by Robert Emmons, professor of psychology at the University of California and Michael McCullough, professor of psychology at the University of Miami, concludes: "Developing a regular gratitude practice is one of the easiest ways to counter the brain's negativity bias—the tendency to cling on to the negative things in our environment. By intentionally focusing on the good parts of our day, the positivity grows. In fact, it only takes 21 days of writing down three things you are grateful for every day to begin reaping the benefits."

The power of gratitude

Clare Law, a writer and mother of two from Kent in the UK, is an advocate of noting down three things. She has long been a believer in the power of gratitude, having started her *Three Beautiful Things* online gratitude blog.

Initially, she says, it began in reaction to the number of negative blogs she had encountered. "I was reading some really cynical and downbeat posts and knew I wanted a more positive response to life," she explains. "My premise was simple—to compile a written record of just three things I might have seen, heard, or experienced during that day that had given me pleasure."

Uplifting experience

Authenticity was important to Law from the word go. "Although my blog was posted online, I wrote only for myself, not for any imagined audience," she says. "But it was really rewarding when people started to come back to me to say they'd appreciated the same things that had moved me. I'm not a permanently cheerful person, so I had to work quite hard sometimes to find things I was grateful for. Often, it came down to sensory experiences—things I'd cooked and enjoyed eating, plants I'd seen during a walk in the park."

How does Law feel the experience of keeping her online gratitude journal improved her quality of life? "The process of writing each post was uplifting in itself, but I also found it particularly comforting to look back on my journal and realize that good things happened, even on days that had seemed to be particularly tough. Additional spins-offs included encountering a whole range of like-minded people online, plus the discipline of making myself write every day undoubtedly improved my work."

Law's blog took her through the journey of her adult life including the start of her career, marriage, and the birth of her children. "I only stopped blogging online because my children had reached an age where I felt I shouldn't be talking about them in the public domain. After 10 years of recording my gratitude, though, it's an ingrained habit, and I still mentally note the small things that give me pleasure on a regular basis."

Can you think of three things that went well today? Was there anything you did to make these things happen?

▶ ....

....

▶ ....

....

▶ ....

....

Attach a picture of something or someone that you feel grateful for.

Keep a gratitude journal

Four tips to get you started...

- Try to write something every day. Keep it simple, don't overthink it, and don't worry about creating poetry—just get it down on the page.

- If you don't manage to write something daily, don't beat yourself up about it—it's supposed to be a pleasure, not a chore. Concentrate on what you have managed to write and not what you haven't.

- Getting the best from your journal is all about authenticity—you're not writing for an audience, but for yourself. "Surviving a horrible day" is something to be grateful for in itself.

- Don't forget to read back over your journal regularly—it's a great way to remind yourself that even dull or difficult times have high points.

"Fill your paper with the breathings of your heart."

William Wordsworth

Today I am grateful for...

Monday

➤ ....
....

➤ ....
....

➤ ....
....

➤ ....
....

➤ ....
....

➤ ....
....

➤ ....
....

➤ ....
....

Today I am grateful for...

Tuesday

➤ ....
....

➤ ....
....

➤ ....
....

➤ ....
....

➤ ....
....

➤ ....
....

➤ ....
....

➤ ....
....

Today I am grateful for...

Wednesday

▶ ....

....

▶ ....

....

▶ ....

....

▶ ....

....

▶ ....

....

▶ ....

....

▶ ....

....

▶ ....

....

Today I am grateful for...

Thursday

➤ ....
....

➤ ....
....

➤ ....
....

➤ ....
....

➤ ....
....

➤ ....
....

➤ ....
....

➤ ....
....

Today I am grateful for...

Friday

➤ ....
....

➤ ....
....

➤ ....
....

➤ ....
....

➤ ....
....

➤ ....
....

➤ ....
....

Today I am grateful for...

Saturday

▶ ....
....

▶ ....
....

▶ ....
....

▶ ....
....

▶ ....
....

▶ ....
....

▶ ....
....

▶ ....
....

Today I am grateful for...

Sunday

➤ ....

....

➤ ....

....

➤ ....

....

➤ ....

....

➤ ....

....

➤ ....

....

➤ ....

....

➤ ....

....

A head full of worries

Micromanaging every event can bring a sense of control, but it won't stop you fretting and it can't guarantee everything will go to plan. In fact, it might just mean you miss the main event—life.

If you are a worrier, chances are you prefer to have things planned out and know what's happening—where, when, how, and with whom. You like to have covered every possibility, rehearsed conversations in your mind, explored the full range of scenarios, and be sure you know how those involved will react. In this way, you are in control, which means you can stop worrying. Or does it?

Planning to the *nth* degree doesn't stop you worrying

It's understandable why you might think it should. If you're nervous of social situations where you don't know who's attending, for instance, it can be a cause of much anxiety. You figure that if you can find out this information then you'll no longer be nervous. But what if the expected people cancel and others arrive in their place? How will that make you feel? And what will you do?

The worry might even be at home. Perhaps you're relinquishing the oven mitts and giving in to your partner's request to cook dinner. You know what they're making, they have all the ingredients and the recipe, and they can call on you if they get stuck. But if they do something wrong and the dinner is inedible, what will you eat? What if they make a mess and you have to clean it up? Or what if they don't prepare the dish properly and you get food poisoning? You have a presentation to deliver tomorrow, you can't be ill.

There's always a "What if?"

It doesn't matter how much you plan, prepare, and rehearse for a situation so that any worries you have are covered, there's always the unexpected. You may have thought and prepared for ten outcomes, but then "What if?" pipes up with an 11th version. You could plan for 1,000 variables in a situation but "What if?" will still find another.

And then you're back to square one, worrying again. Why is this? Because you want to feel in control and believe that if you are in control then everything and everyone will be okay. The trouble is, maintaining complete control is impossible. Not simply improbable, it's impossible. Situations, people, and outcomes cannot be controlled—by you or anyone else. That's hard to accept. It's difficult to admit you can't keep everyone safe, that you can't guarantee what someone's reaction will be, that you don't know what's going to happen.

The tighter you try to grip on to control, with the intention of pacifying your worries, the less likely you are to find peace. You put so much time, thought, and energy into managing what's happening, trying to anticipate changes and worrying about the "What ifs?," that you aren't fully a part of what's going on around you. And once an event is over and your worries turned out to be unfounded, you realize you missed out on the fun because you were too busy holding on so tightly.

You end up feeling exhausted, let down by the actions you thought would help you, and fed up that you spent more energy worrying than you did enjoying yourself or simply being part of it all.

What about those around you?

How does this desire to control—in the name of keeping people safe and happy, of completing work, of being responsible, of making sure things are okay and nothing goes wrong—affect the people you love, work with, or spend time with?

In the process of wanting to feel in control it's easy to feel the need to know what other people are doing, where they're going and when, how they're going to think, feel, act, or react. If that doesn't fit in with what you believe needs to happen for everything to be okay, then there can be the tendency to want to exert control over them, too. Not in a sinister, threatening, take-away-your-liberty way—you want what's best for them and for everyone, after all—but in a way that might be unwelcome nonetheless.

It's quite possible, for instance, that your friends, family, or colleagues might not appreciate being micromanaged. Think of it in reverse. How would you feel if you knew you were being controlled by another person, even a small amount, irrespective of whether their motive springs from a desire to protect and care for you?

The fact is you can never be in complete control. But going in the opposite direction isn't helpful either. So, what can you do?

Ways to worry less

Recognize your need for control.

First of all, learn to recognize what you're doing. Look out for the signs that you are overthinking and overplanning. Do you really need to know all the details? Are you trying to second-guess people? Are you creating multiple possible scenarios and are you trying to influence others by stealth? Establish why you need to have everything planned.

Ask yourself why you need to plan and counterplan to the *nth* degree—and be honest. You do not need to admit it to anyone else, but you do need to be truthful with yourself.

Record your thoughts here.

....

....

....

....

....

....

....

....

....

....

....

....

....

....

....

Practice self-kindness

Now give yourself a break and practice self-compassion. You are not a bad person, you are not trying to play puppeteer, and you don't want to be controlling. You worry, you want what is best for everyone, and your intentions are good. Worrying this much is no fun, you do not want to spend so much time overthinking, and you do not want to micromanage other people. Be kind to yourself, this is difficult.

Begin to loosen the grip

- Once you are aware that your worrying is leading you to try to control a situation—and you have decided this is not how you want to feel or act—you can begin to let go of the reins.

- You know deep down that you cannot plan for every possible outcome, so bring it into the light and tell yourself that.

- You know that trying to be in control does not make you worry any less. It is hard to admit but you know it to be true.

- You know that you have managed, coped with, and survived every unexpected and unplanned event and situation that life has thrown at you so far, because here you are today.

- You know that relinquishing a little of that need to be in control does not mean your life will fall apart. It means that you—and not your worry—are in control of your own life, as you have known all along.

"What if you fall? Oh, but my darling, what if you fly?"

Erin Hanson

Learn to trust yourself

Stop planning and start smiling.

A need for control often stems from fear. "What if something goes wrong?" or "What if I don't know what to say?" Learning to trust that you will be fine, and that things will work out, is the answer. But how do you do this?

By not planning something that normally you would. Start small, and see what happens. A regular meeting, perhaps? Or a weekend afternoon?

And if your first experience doesn't turn out well, don't give up. Try again. Go for something even smaller.

Record what happens here.

....

....

....

....

....

....

....

....

....

....

....

....

....

....

....

....

Worrying habit

There are many times in life when worrying might be justified and exerting a degree of control is necessary, but if it is affecting your everyday life, it might be helpful to try the following exercise.

Write down the people or events that are causing you the most concern.

....

....

....

....

....

....

....

....

Explore your reasons and motives behind this anxiety and your need to control the situation.

....

....

....

....

....

....

....

....

....

....

....

....

....

....

Now try to recall occasions when you micromanaged similar events or guided people to a decision. Ask yourself what happened. Was your input welcomed?

....

....

....

....

....

....

....

How did people react to your behavior?

....

....

....

....

....

....

....

Were your fears justified?

....

....

....

....

....

....

....

One thing at a time

Not so long ago, multitasking was necessary for those wishing to get ahead. But it seems the monotaskers may have been working more effectively all along...

Here's a question. How often do you focus on one task, seeing it through from beginning to end, without being distracted? Chances are you are in a permanent state of multitasking—eating lunch while catching up with work emails, walking while texting, or checking Facebook notifications while talking to friends or family.

It's the modern thing—trying to cram a long list of to-dos into don't really have time. For those who seem to manage this feat, this all-dancing, all-singing, plate-spinning, walking-talking ability can become a badge of honor, sitting proudly at the top of their resume.

The reality, however, is that multitasking is an illusion, a myth. It compromises all the activities you think you are doing. According to neuroscientists, the human brain is not wired to handle multiple complex tasks simultaneously. It works best when monotasking, tackling one job at a time. When you think you're multitasking, you're sequential tasking—switching rapidly from one thing to another, a process that makes you less efficient and, ultimately, scatter-brained.

Earl Miller, professor of neuroscience at The Picower Institute for Learning and Memory at the Massachusetts Institute of Technology (MIT) and a world leader on divided attention, explained this in *Fortune*'s Tools of the Trade series. "Humans have a very limited capacity for simultaneous thought and can only hold a little bit of information in the mind at any single moment. When people toggle between tasks, it often feels seamless—but in reality, it requires a series of small shifts."

Each time your brain goes through that switching process, says Professor Miller, "there is a cognitive price to pay"—that price being a loss in productivity and creativity, because you need to expend valuable mental energy refocusing when you return to the activity you interrupted. Switching also drains your creativity. He adds that innovative thinking comes from extended concentration, from being able to follow a thought through a network of new paths. If you are constantly jumping from one thing to another, you will never get far enough down any road to stumble upon your eureka moment.

Room for error

Dr. Daniel Levitin, professor of psychology and neuroscience at Montreal's McGill University and author of *The Organized Mind: Thinking Straight in the Age of Information Overload*, is unequivocal about the effects of trying to keep more than one plate in the air. "Fractionating" your attention means you overload your brain with "separate projects that have separate start times and separate monitoring processes... the neurobiological impact of all that switching is that you deplete the very neurochemicals you need to focus."

Multitasking uses up brain fuel and leaves it running on empty, increasing the likelihood of making mistakes by up to 100 percent (depending on what you're doing). Interruptions of just a couple of seconds, that is the time it takes for a person to scan a text or email, doubled the error rate among a group of 300 participants who were doing sequence-based tests for a 2013 study by Michigan State University.

It makes sense when you think about it. If a computer has too many applications running, the wheel of doom invariably appears, spinning around, leaving the underlying operating system unable to function. That's your brain. Multitasking puts it into the wheel-of-doom mode.

Think about the times you multitask. List them here.

....
....
....
....
....
....
....
....
....
....
....
....
....
....

Steps to more effective monotasking

1 Turn off the tech
A survey by Nottingham Trent University in the UK found that participants checked their phone 85 times a day, amounting to five hours usage. Treat your cellphone as the enemy of monotasking. Switch it off until you are ready for a break or, if you're not prepared to do that, turn off notifications or use an app-blocker.

2 Set aside time to monotask
If you have an important job to do, give yourself enough time to make a decent start on it—at least 15 minutes to begin with and longer as your attention span increases. Think about your day and schedule your monotasking for when you are least likely to be interrupted. It's no good starting a project five minutes before you have to leave the house.

3 Clear your work area
Your physical environment can be as distracting as your virtual one, so keep your workspace clear. Remember your brain has a novelty bias—that new magazine sitting on your desk may be all it needs to lead you astray.

4 Clustertask
Tackle your emails in 15-minute chunks three or four times a day. Professor Nass says checking email has nothing to do with being efficient and all to do with running away from the job in hand, which is bad for your brain. When you clustertask emails, you consolidate the time you would spend answering them individually into one activity, thereby turning emailing from a distraction into a monotask.

5 Take a break or even have a nap
Enough is sometimes enough. If you have reached the limit of your concentration, take a break (that means a walk, a run, or a nap, not going on to Facebook or watching your favorite TV show). Dr Levitin advises taking 15 minutes off every couple of hours to rest and refuel your brain. He states that a 10- or 15-minute nap during the day is roughly equivalent to 90 minutes' extra sleep the night before and potentially raises your effective IQ by 10 points.

be happy

SLEEP
LESS
DREAM
MORE

How to set some goals you can stick to

The key to making sustainable changes is to start small—setting yourself flashy, New Year-style resolutions seldom works out. Follow these simple rules and give yourself every chance of success.

Choose your battles

You may feel the need to save the world and change drastically, but making too many promises means you are more likely to fail, which can easily discourage you from fulfilling the most important ones. Choose one or two meaningful resolutions to focus on and write them here.

Set your goals

Define your primary goal. Make it specific and realistic by simply devising an action plan so you can break it down into small, concrete steps with short deadlines. Try not to say, for example: "I want to be healthier," but instead "I want to exercise more." However, exercising is the means, not the goal. Your goal could be being able to run a 5k race, swim 10 lengths at your local pool, or learn how to waltz or jive. Once established, you can work out your way to success—like increasing your running time week after week—getting accustomed to each new habit before taking on the next one.

Writing your goal here not only fixes it in your subconscious, but also allows you to record your journey with its ups and downs. As you revisit this journal at a later stage, you can appreciate your efforts, which encourages you to persevere until the goal is accomplished.

Record your goal here.

....

....

....

....

....

....

....

....

....

....

....

....

....

....

....

....

Redefine failure

Accept that you may revert to your old habits, but treat it as a setback and not a failure. If you don't give yourself the time or the chance, a simple stumble can become a good reason to give up.

Don't feel defeated by the first hurdle, be forgiving of yourself, and expect to fall back sometimes. Actually, be proud of each step forward and don't feel it is a failure not to fully achieve your goal.

Record each step you make toward achieving your goal, however small.

....

....

....

....

....

....

....

....

....

....

....

....

....

....

....

....

....

....

Don't set the same goal twice without changing your strategy

Why do people keep failing to reach their goals time after time? Simply because they don't change the habits that sabotage them. They act the same way without learning from their previous failures. So if you didn't succeed the first time, you need to analyze why you didn't reach your goal. If you persist a second time in the same way, you start the vicious cycle of failed attempts and intensify your sense of failure.

Reasons why you didn't reach your goal.

Previous goal ....
....
....
....
....
....
....
....
....

Reasons it wasn't achieved ....
....
....
....
....
....
....
....
....
....

Resolutions can be made any day of the year

Don't make a resolution just because it's the end of the year and it's tradition.
A new year may not necessarily be the right time for you. You need to be mentally
ready to change, and your personal experience and circumstances must lead you
to take the decision to finally do so.

When you are ready, record the precise moment here. What inspired it? Use this
decisive point to motivate you, and to give yourself the necessary push for the
old you to become the new you.

If at first you don't succeed...

Holding on to positivity when all seems lost can yield against-the-odds results—and build resilience.

Would you judge yourself to be someone for whom the glass is always half empty or are you a glass-half-full type? Do you tend to look on the bright side when things don't go according to plan or beat yourself up mercilessly, throwing in the towel and telling yourself that trying again is pointless? Psychological studies have demonstrated that positivity increases well-being, improves health and strengthens relationships. Since the 1950s, an entire self-help genre has been urging people to embrace positivity as the key to happiness. Norman Vincent Peale's *The Power of Positive Thinking* stayed on *The New York Times* bestseller list for 186 consecutive weeks and was translated into 15 languages. But is it really as simple as talking the talk until you can walk the walk? Why is it that some people are better than others at not allowing a first-time failure to stop them from trying again?

Identifying negative self-beliefs

There is an inevitable ebb and flow to life that includes times when things don't go as planned. You can't always prevent them from happening, but you can think about how to respond. It may seem as if thoughts and feelings that arise are purely instinctive, just part of who you are, but seeing that there are choices in how to respond to any life situation can help encourage more flexible and creative solutions that shift entrenched beliefs: *"I never do well," "Things always go wrong in my life," "I always make a fool of myself."* These statements latch on like sticky burrs, encouraging a negative state of mind from the outset, which then influences the likelihood of giving up and builds toward a self-fulfilling prophecy.

Think back to the last time something didn't turn out the way you wanted it to.

What was your response?

How could you have responded more positively?

119

Celebrating the good, letting go of the bad

Being able to hold on to positivity is about more than repeating positive mantras until they start to stick. Acquiring enough resilience is also essential to coping with setbacks when things seem beyond reach and self-esteem has dropped into a dark hole. It could be that there is something about accepting those setbacks, and the difficult feelings that accompany them, that enables positivity to enter the arena and foster renewed intent.

In 2012, a 10-year study by Hal E. Hershfield et al tracked the emotional state of San Francisco residents. Researchers found that those who often felt a mixture of positive and negative emotions, or taking the good with the bad, enjoyed better health than those who generally felt just positive. An important factor is to learn to observe negative feelings through meditation and mindfulness techniques, which reduces their sting and allows them to pass.

Practice this exercise

When a negative thought enters your mind, take a moment to acknowledge it, and notice how it makes you feel. Now thank the thought, and allow it to float past, like a cloud. Just let it go. Don't agree or disagree. Just be aware of it, then—"Okay, thanks thought, goodbye."

Remember.
You can't stop thoughts, but you can choose how to respond to them.

"You may encounter many defeats, but you must not be defeated. In fact, it may be necessary to encounter the defeats, so you can know who you are, what you can rise from, how you can still come out of it."
Maya Angelou

Building resilience

When thinking about emotional resilience, psychotherapists point to a complex interplay of experiences during childhood as crucial to how people make sense of the world; and, critically, how they equip themselves to cope with the difficulties that life throws up. Recalling when you first learned to ride a bike without stabilizers can help illustrate a pivotal moment in the building of your own resilience—the ability to dig deep and keep going until you get there.

Young children internalize such messages, absorbing them as mantras or life scripts for adulthood. In these moments, a negative comment can feel crushing, just as positive encouragement—*"Look at you. Well done, you're almost there"*—can make all the difference.

Can you recall a time when you found something difficult but kept going until you mastered it?

One step at a time

"If at first you don't succeed try, try and try again." Robert the Bruce, King of Scotland, is meant to have said this to rally his troops shortly before their triumph against the English in 1314. The idiom, said to have been inspired by a humble spider stoically weaving his web as Bruce hid from his English pursuers in a cave, encourages everyone to reach inside themselves and see if they can come up with something new next time they're up against it, grappling with despondency and despair.

When the chips are down, it's easy to feel that others have all the luck, life is unfair, so what's the point in trying? But accepting feelings of loss and sadness, not beating yourself up and drawing on resilience to give it another go can allow the successes—however small—not only to be up for grabs, but perhaps even sweeter.

Write from the heart

How often do you resist the urge to tell someone what you really think or feel? What if you could share your feelings in a safe place? Welcome to Notes I'll Never Send...

Writing honestly, without fear of judgment, is one of the best forms of emotional and spiritual release. Expressing in written form an upsetting incident or argument can help you to set it free, close an unhappy chapter of your life, and move on.

Notes I'll Never Send is a way of addressing an inconsiderate friend, an intransigent boss, an adulterous spouse, a lost parent, or a demanding child, even a compassionate stranger.

Whatever the reason you feel the need to "talk" to this person—fear, anger, love, jealousy, a need for space—this is a way to get to the heart of the issue. And knowing the addressee will never read your note allows you to write honestly and without prejudice. This is not about them. It is about you. Without having to protect their feelings, or skirt around issues to save face, you are completely free to share your innermost thoughts and feelings.

And this process of putting your thoughts into words—by externalizing them—can be extremely rewarding. It liberates you from the hurt, worry, anxiety, or regret as you transfer your feelings from the internal to the external and get them out of your system.

Release your feelings

Think of the design of your note. There is no right or wrong format, but your choices can add to its significance. It's not just whimsy you're dashing off. You are putting time, thought, and effort into it. You could use the final pages of your journal, or buy a postcard and decorate it using images or patterns that are relevant to the issue. You can use anything—paint, markers, collage, fabric, photographs, magazine articles, dried flowers, or leaves—the only person it has to please is you.

The words, meanwhile, should express your feelings in the most honest way possible. Be as candid as you can. As it is a note rather than a letter, you need to be quite concise. Think about what it is you really want to say, express the core feelings that are causing you disquiet or unhappiness, and commit to paper with candor. It could be a handful of carefully chosen words, a couple of sentences, or a long paragraph that fills the space. However much—or little—you write, the sense of release can be immeasurable.

STERLING
New York

An Imprint of Sterling Publishing Co., Inc.
1166 Avenue of the Americas
New York, NY 10036

STERLING and the distinctive Sterling logo are registered trademarks of Sterling Publishing Co., Inc.
BREATHE is a trademark of The Guild of Master Craftsman Publications Ltd

ISBN 978-1-4549-3450-9

Distributed in Canada by Sterling Publishing Co., Inc.
c/o Canadian Manda Group, 664 Annette Street
Toronto, Ontario M6S 2C8, Canada

For information about custom editions, special sales, and premium and corporate purchases, please
contact Sterling Special Sales at 800-805-5489 or specialsales@sterlingpublishing.com.

Manufactured in China

8 10 9 7

sterlingpublishing.com

Cover illustration: Anieszka Banks
Illustrations and photographs: Shutterstock.com, Alamy.com, Stephanie Hofmann

Publisher: Jonathan Grogan, Designer: Jo Chapman
Compiled by Susie Duff
Editorial: Catherine Kielthy, Jane Roe
Words credits: Jo Bisseker Barr, Arabella Black, Karen Bray, Lorna Cowan, Tracy Hallett,
Katie Holloway, Jennifer Hudson, Juliana Kassianos, Anna Lambert, Marissa Peer, Amy Schofield,
Gabrielle Treanor, Janette Wolf